FALL IN LOVE
WITH MONDAY MORNINGS

♥

*The Career Woman's
Guide to Increasing
Impact, Influence,
and Income*

Nadine Haupt

INDIE BOOKS
INTERNATIONAL

ISBN: 1-941870-27-9
ISBN 13: 978-1-941870-27-3
Library of Congress Control Number: 2015939224

Designed by Joni McPherson, mcphersongraphics.com

INDIE BOOKS INTERNATIONAL, LLC
2424 VISTA WAY, SUITE 316
OCEANSIDE, CA 92054

www.indiebooksintl.com

Dedication

To Dad, Mom, Heather, and my co-pilot Lucy

CONTENTS

CHAPTER ONE

The OGIM (Oh God, It's Monday) Syndrome

Look at the bright side. At least Mondays only happen once a week.

GARFIELD THE CAT

There is an epidemic emerging throughout Corporate America and business worldwide. It targets high achieving, results-driven, mid-career women by stalling their advancement and threatening their success. The symptoms are many, and can strike at any time. Typically, sufferers don't see it coming. The disease can incubate for months, even years, before exposing itself in devastating and debilitating fashion. It's called "Oh God, It's Monday Syndrome."

Most commonly referred to as OGIM, the disease begins as a conscious effort to follow the advice and path of other successful individuals. What creates a problem, however, is the path leads to a bleak destination that's molded by outside influences instead of internal motivation. OGIM affects not only career performance and advancement, but also other significant areas of life: personal relationships, health, wellness, finances, and social life. At its worst, OGIM can hijack a person's entire life, stealing joy and happiness right out from underneath them.

The symptoms are common and easy to recognize:

▶ **Lost the drive to get up and go to the office.** Every morning becomes a battle between you and the snooze button. Before losing your drive, you leaped out of bed eager to attack the day ahead. Now you struggle to get the motivation to brush your teeth after your morning coffee.

▶ **Working harder and longer hours but don't seem to be getting ahead.** Forget the forty-hour workweek. You are lucky if you only clock sixty hours. Your work load keeps increasing while your pay stagnates. Shifts in business downsize your department, and you are saddled with more and more responsibilities with fewer and fewer people to help. A promotion or a raise? Yeah, right.

▶ **Discouraged on whether change is possible.** They say the grass is greener on the other side, but you are highly skeptical. All business is the same. Your peers at other companies face the same struggles you do, so why would you think it should be different anywhere else? Even if you had the opportunity to change, you doubt if it's reasonable to expect a higher position, more money, passion, and career satisfaction.

▶ **Frustrated at the lack of advancement opportunities.** When you first started your career, advancement was fast and furious. It felt like opportunity existed everywhere you looked. Now, moving up the career ladder feels the same as watching paint dry before you can apply the next coat. Problem is, the paint is thick and doesn't seem to be drying at all. So, you wait and wait. After all, the color is nice, just not perfect.

▶ **Increased stress and anxiety about the future.** You blame the extra caffeine in the coffee or your sugar jolt in the afternoon for your anxiety attacks. Stress levels continue to increase as you ponder the fact what you're doing now may be your long-term future if you don't take action to change something.

▶ **Feeling under-utilized, unappreciated, battle weary, and burnt out.** You know you have much more to offer, but no one seems to care. The stellar work you have accomplished has gone unnoticed. You picked and fought so many battles you have lost count of your win-loss percentage. You tell yourself to just keep your armor up because everyone is out to capture more territory at the expense of others. Co-workers are backstabbing one another. At this point, why bother to fight? Whatever you do, nothing makes a difference in getting your work noticed.

▶ **Sensing that you are trapped in current circumstances.** You have responsibilities—a spouse, kids, a mortgage (or two), car loans, student loans, saving for college, saving for retirement, lots and lots of bills. The list goes on. At least you know the devil you are dealing with. You feel it's impossible to make any career changes because of the financial load you carry. It's becoming more and more difficult to tap into your dreams.

▶ **Yearn to make a bigger impact, for your voice to be heard, and to get your groove back taking on work that energizes you.** Deep down inside, you know you are meant for greater things. There is still a fire in your belly—a desire—to do more, be more, and have more. The hunger and longing is there. You possess a vision of greatness, creating success on your terms, being your own boss. You just don't know how to get out of the OGIM funk.

Sunday Night Blues

For many with OGIM Syndrome, the symptoms flare up on Sunday evenings. After a weekend of fun with family and friends, when the clock strikes 5 pm on Sunday night, your energy level noticeably shifts.

Tomorrow is Monday. The harsh realization that in fewer than twelve hours you have to get up and go back to work that drains you starts to settle in. Slowly the joy and happiness you had over the weekend begins to turn to anxiety. You ruminate about the five days of agony ahead of you. Tension builds in your body. Stress occupies your mind.

As you are washing the dishes from dinner, your four-year-old daughter bounds into the kitchen. She beams you a smile as she holds up her favorite toy asking you to play with her. Your mind is preoccupied. You don't hear her. She continues to plead with you, "Mommy, play with me—please." When you finally hear her little voice, as sweet as it is, it sounds like yet another demand on your time. The stress and anxiety about the week ahead rushes over you. You lash out, "*No. Can't you see I'm busy?*" Her beautiful smile turns upside down as she drops her head and slowly walks away. You stop washing the pot in your hand—the water continues to run in the sink. Immediately you wish you could take back that moment, and you realize something has to change.

Dishes are done, but feelings of despair continue to build within you. You move into your go-to avoidance technique—either watching mindless television or attempting to get lost in a book. You curl up on the couch. Your heart is racing, and your shoulders feel tight. How can you relieve the tension? Sleep seems impossible, so you reach for a glass of wine to ease the strain. That glass becomes two, then three, until you finish off the bottle. Dread for Monday morning.

You ask yourself, *What happened? How in the world did I get here? This isn't what I wanted or expected.* Monday morning depression is negatively impacting other aspects of your life. You can't deny it anymore. Your relationships are suffering. Your family is on edge. Your finances are a mess. You have no social life. You've gained weight and lost the energy to engage in the activities you love. You desperately want things to be different, but you just don't know where to start.

You're not alone.

In 2013, the Gallup Organization released the report "State of the American Workplace" based on data collected over the previous five years. Of the approximately one hundred million people in America who hold full-time jobs, seventy million workers are not engaged, meaning that the vast majority is not reaching their fullest potential. The majority of people in the workplace are just plain checked out. Studies have shown workers who are disengaged and emotionally detached from their work are less likely to be productive. Obviously this creates a considerable negative impact on a company's bottom line, but it also impacts an individual's bottom line. When business struggles, its employees struggle as well. Financially, the impact on the employee's bottom line appears as stagnating wages, no profit sharing or bonuses, and certainly no advancement opportunities.

Business cultures unknowingly escalate the problem when they allow groups of disengaged employees to congregate. Negative thoughts swirl throughout an organization, pulling individuals down further. At its worst, the culture can implode vigorously into a swirl of gossip, conflict, and contempt. News outlets focused on fear-based reporting add fuel to the fire with reports of financial collapse, despair, and constant worry about fluctuating markets. As an individual, it becomes more and more difficult to step outside these strong forces. Eventually, you find yourself backed into a corner with no foreseeable way out of the stress.

Perhaps you listened to your peers and well-meaning mentors to help you chart your career path. Each step did bring some form of success, but not fulfillment. Even with the financial benefits, you know deep down where you are in your career now is not where you want to be. You might have been able to deal with the situation for a while, but eventually OGIM Syndrome consumes your Sunday nights and leaks into every day of the week. It is costing you emotionally, mentally, financially, and even physically. You feel stuck trying to make the best of things as they are in your life.

Do not lose hope. There is a way out. OGIM Syndrome is a temporary condition that can be reversed. You know you are destined for greater things, but you just don't know where to start. I can help you. How do I know? I've been there—multiple times.

In the next chapter I will tell my story in more detail, but as a woman in a male-dominated industry, I often found myself stuck and held back by circumstances outside my control. But over the years I found ways to push through these road blocks and my feelings of disengagement. Remember that this won't always be a one-time fix—the symptoms can resurface throughout your career and you may have to jumpstart yourself again. Equipping yourself with the proper tools will make this process easier each time. For me, every time I shifted my mindset in this way, it resulted in my succeeding in creating opportunities, building influence, increasing my income substantially, and falling in love with Monday mornings again.

▶ FUEL FOR THOUGHT ◀

- Oh God It's Monday (OGIM) Syndrome is a common affliction affecting high-achieving, results-driven, mid-career women by stalling their career advancement and threatening their success.

- Symptoms include discouragement, frustration, despair, and feeling under-utilized, unappreciated, and burnt out.

- OGIM Syndrome affects more than just your career. It impacts your personal relationships, finances, health and wellness, and social life.

CHAPTER TWO

You Can Accelerate Out of the Slow Lane and Win

Don't be afraid to give up the good to go for the great.

JOHN D. ROCKEFELLER

If you are experiencing OGIM Syndrome, please know that your situation and circumstances are not unusual. You are simply joining the many others who have found themselves stuck and discouraged and wondering how they got to a place of despair. It feels like you just keep spinning your wheels. Previously, you found a way to get traction and continue to advance. But for some reason, this time is different.

Maybe it's increased personal responsibilities or external changes that make you feel lost and not in control. It's important you realize that changing gears to spark advancement again in your career is possible. You have a choice—remain in the slow lane, or find a way to accelerate into the fast lane.

If you are going to continue to play small, stay in your comfort zone, and hold on to one of your many excuses about why things will never change, you might as well stop reading this book right now. You are not going to like what I have to say. But if you are eager to find the remedy to OGIM Syndrome, let's keep going.

My Story

Before you and I get down to business, you need to know a little bit about me. Over twenty years ago, as one of the few women in my freshman mechanical engineering class at Purdue University, I began a journey as a pioneer for women in male-dominated industries. Of course I didn't realize it at the time. All I knew was that I wanted to work on cars—*fast* cars.

Maybe it was the influence of my childhood playing with Hot Wheels and watching the Indianapolis 500 every Memorial Day weekend. Perhaps it was the excitement of learning to drive a manual transmission with my dad in his 1979 MGB convertible. Nevertheless, when the opportunity came to spend the summer working as an engineering intern in engine design on the original Dodge Viper V10 engine, I didn't hesitate.

After graduating Purdue, I joined Chrysler and got a master's degree in mechanical engineering. I secured a position in the Motorsports group at Chrysler—which was actually in marketing at the time—but quickly discovered (my first experience with OGIM Syndrome) that I longed for a more technical, hands-on role. That's when I took a huge risk, leaving the so-called security of Corporate America, to become the first female trackside engine engineer in Championship Auto Racing Teams (CART)/IndyCar racing.

During the next seven years I orchestrated moves within racing's Good Ol' Boys' Network to work for three engine manufacturers (Honda, Mercedes-Ilmor, and Ford-Cosworth) while supporting over eight different race teams and multiple drivers. ESPN, local television news stations, and newspapers across the globe were eager to interview the woman who successfully paved the way for women in the technical aspects of professional auto racing.

It was a blast, but eventually, the day came where heading out to the racetrack at 5:00 am was no longer fun. The travel—national and international—was grueling. We went from an eight-month season to a full twelve-month season of race events and testing. I grew tired of living out of a suitcase and not having much of a life outside work. Politics and egos were complicating my life as well. That's when I decided to take another big calculated risk (my second OGIM Syndrome event).

I walked away from my lucrative job in motorsports to get an MBA from Pepperdine University, move back to Chicago, and take a position at an engineering consulting firm focused on product liability. Yep, I walked right into yet another significantly male-dominated industry. In fact, I was the only female engineer at the firm. A few years later I got restless and left to become the manager of strategic planning at Navistar's Engine Group (my third OGIM Syndrome encounter).

While I was at Navistar (aka International Truck and Engine—yet another male-dominated industry of commercial trucking and engine engineering), I pursued a direction not fully supported by many executives at the company. I felt we needed to investigate the future of alternative fuels. It was a big risk career-wise, but it paid off. I became a well-known expert and speaker in the industry, and my influence at Navistar increased significantly. For a while it appeared as though I had finally reached my ultimate career position, but something still wasn't right. I realized that I'd spent my whole life as a passenger in someone else's car (my fourth OGIM syndrome episode).

In other words, I was born to be an entrepreneur.

Once I figured that out, I hired a coach to help me integrate all the different parts of me (the technical part, the business part, and the creative part) in a way that would allow me to be the most successful and fulfilled—and make the biggest difference in the world—in a way that was 100 percent unique to me.

That's when F.A.S.T. Women in Business was born, and I haven't looked back.

A F.A.S.T. Woman?

"Just what exactly do you mean by F.A.S.T.?" you ask.

I'm so glad you asked.

Being **F.A.S.T.** is all about being **Fearless, Ambitious, Strong,** and **Trailblazing** your way to success. The following traits show you what it takes to become a F.A.S.T. Woman in Business.

▶ **Committed to winning, but not at any cost.** I'm referring to a commitment to excellence, not sleeping your way to the top. Being in alignment with your values and making choices based on your priorities will drive success on your terms. Knowing your priorities is the key to lasting change and fulfillment in your career.

▶ **Fueled by passion and driven by a dream.** It's time to stop extinguishing the flame burning deep inside. For years you pushed aside your dream, deeming it unreachable or not the right timing. Tap into your passion and zest for life. Fully embrace your inner motivation. Stop dreaming your dream and start *living it.*

▶ **Supported by a pit crew like no other.** Initiating, creating, and sustaining lasting change cannot be undertaken alone. You need an amazing and successful support team to encourage, push, stretch, and guide you to new heights. Going it alone is a struggle. Construct the right team around you, and success will arrive faster and easier.

Each time I found myself suffering from OGIM Syndrome and longing to make a change in my career, I went through a process to re-engage and develop a strategy for action. First, I had to overcome my inner obstacles before tackling the external roadblocks. I took inventory of where I was and where I wanted to go. By staying in alignment with my intention and motivation, I constructed a strategy and action plan to build the right network, increase my influence, take calculated risks, and reinvent myself multiple times. What I realized was it was these F.A.S.T. traits that I consistently embraced to propel myself forward, push past my comfort zone, and successfully advance my career.

I'm telling you all this because it seems everyone is quick to try and give you advice. However, they haven't earned the right. Be very careful about who you let mentor, coach, and guide you. I'm not going to judge you, put you down, or make you feel you can't do something. That's up to you. But I am going to challenge you. I'm going to inspire you to do more, be more, and have more. Because that's what being a F.A.S.T. Woman in Business is all about!

Deep down you know *exactly* what you want. Sometimes, those desires of yours don't match up to the expectations of others. Your definition of success may be wildly different from another's. This is why women need a community of like-minded visionaries—passionate and bold women who break the mold cast by society and instead blaze their own trail to success. Each woman's journey is unique and constantly evolving.

Famous F.A.S.T. Women

It would be hard to imagine a F.A.S.T. Woman and not think of Oprah Winfrey. After a difficult and tumultuous childhood, Winfrey took Chicago by storm in January 1984 as the host of *AM Chicago*, a low-rated, half-hour morning talk show. I recall my own mother watching this young black woman on morning television with equal amounts of intrigue and bewilderment. After all, Phil Donahue was the national king of talk shows in an industry dominated by white males, which made a woman host a real curiosity.

Within months after Winfrey took over, *AM Chicago* went from the ratings basement to overtake *Donahue* as Chicago's top rated talk show. By September 1986, the show was renamed *The Oprah Winfrey Show*, expanded to a full hour, and broadcast nationally. Her syndicated show toppled Donahue's national audience and his hold on the number-one daytime talk show in America.

This F.A.S.T. Woman is credited with creating a more intimate, emotional, and conversational form of media communication. TV commentator Howard Rosenberg said, "She's a roundhouse, a full-course meal, big, brassy, loud, aggressive, hyper, laughable, loveable, soulful, tender, low-down, earthy, and hungry." I don't think I could define the essence of a F.A.S.T. Woman better myself.

There are examples of famous F.A.S.T. Women in Business everywhere you look, such as Suze Orman in the area of financial services. Sara Blakely, founder of SPANX, is the world's youngest self-made female billionaire. Mary Barra, CEO of General Motors, became the first women ever to head a Big Eight automaker. Barbara Corcoran turned $1,000 into a billion-dollar business in real estate. These famous examples are meant to inspire you to push past your comfort zone. Find and fuel your own passion, and create your own definition of success.

Why Become a F.A.S.T. Woman

Many years ago, I went out to Los Angeles to celebrate a close friend's milestone birthday. Walking through the terminal at LAX after the flight from Chicago, my eye was caught by an advertisement on the wall. For the life of me, I don't remember what the ad was selling, but the statement made a significant impact on my life.

"Do what you *want*, not what you *can*."

At the time, I was struggling in a job that was uninspiring. I wanted to leverage my MBA and get out of engineering. The two-and-a-half-year relationship with my boyfriend had stalled. It seemed like my entire life was slipping into the OGIM Syndrome. When I returned from that trip, I knew it was time to take action. Armed with a new perspective, I led with what I *wanted* to do and let go of the self-imposed limitations of what I *could* do. My life began to change.

You can change your life too. By becoming a F.A.S.T. Woman in Business, you create the career and life you truly desire. You find a way to fuel your passion. As your energy shifts, you attract wealth and abundance in all areas of your life—professional *and* personal. Throughout the process, you build unwavering confidence and fearlessness while enhancing your influence as a leader. By gaining clarity and laser focus, you are able to realize your full potential and define success on your terms. Most of all, you live life adventurously and surround yourself with an inner circle of champions who continually lift you to new summits. Imagine a life and career where possibilities and opportunities are endless.

Are you in? Eager to join the F.A.S.T. Women in Business community? Ladies, start your engines, and proceed to the starting line in chapter 3. The time has come to break through your inner glass ceiling.

▶ FUEL FOR THOUGHT ◀

- You can overcome OGIM Syndrome and create amazing results in your career and life.

- Being F.A.S.T. is all about being Fearless, Ambitious, Strong, and Trailblazing your way to success on your terms.

- "Do what you *want*, not what you *can*." What does that mean for you? You get to decide.

CHAPTER THREE

Break Through Your Inner Glass Ceiling

Have the courage to follow your heart and intuition. They somehow already know what you truly want to become. Everything else is secondary.

STEVE JOBS

A ny woman who has spent time in Corporate America has at least heard of the term glass ceiling. Most likely, if you are a high achiever within the corporate environment, you have bumped into it at some point in your career.

The glass ceiling is often described as an invisible barrier that prevents women from moving further up the corporate ladder. The level at which this glass ceiling appears differs among industries. In predominately male-dominated disciplines such as science, engineering, and technology, this ceiling can be quite low. From this vantage point below the glass ceiling, a woman may be able to see the high-level corporate position but she is effectively kept from achieving it as a result of this invisible barrier. While the corporate glass ceiling may be contributing to the slowdown of career advancement, there is a more potent barrier that stops women. It is called the "inner glass ceiling."

The foundation for any successful and lasting change starts with the right mindset. In motor racing, preparation was the key to winning. In between race weekends, race teams would go testing to further develop the car and gather data to prepare for the next race. The chief engineer would develop a test plan to make small, subtle changes to the car to gauge the effect on performance. Besides looking at the data collected during a run, the team also relied heavily on driver feedback to add that subjective input on the changes. A change that works for one driver does not necessarily work for another, depending on the individual's driving style and approach.

Typically, test days were very long, often twelve to sixteen hours. We would make changes to the car, run a few laps, debrief what we observed, and then make more adjustments. Unfortunately, there would be occasions during test days when the subjective feedback from the driver would be difficult, if not impossible, to obtain. Why? The driver wasn't focused on the testing because his mind was elsewhere: family troubles, concerns over bills, dreaming of an upcoming vacation, or some other pressing thing in his life. As a result, the feedback would be contradicting or nonexistent. After what would seem like the hundredth change to the car with no apparent improvement, the mechanics would start to joke in the garage and say, "You gotta work on the nut behind the wheel before your go fixin' the bolts on the car." In other words, the driver has to get focused and clear on the objectives of the test, otherwise all the changes the team keeps making on the car are a huge waste of time.

Whether we are talking about a racecar driver during a test or a woman contemplating a significant career change, everything starts with the right mindset. Each time I begin work with a new client, I introduce her to my Success Factor Mindset Model: Awareness—Attitude—Action.

You need to be focused and clear about who you are, where you are heading, and possess the right attitude before launching an action plan. Without these elements, you can keep making all the changes you want in your outer world, but the results will remain the same. To make lasting change successful, you have to work from the inside out.

My philosophy is that lasting change will only occur when you first identify who you are at your core by understanding your values, talents, motivators, and deepest desires. Getting super clear on your core thoughts and beliefs will allow you to be able to push through your doubts and fears and take the right actions. This is how you work from the inside out. Address the inner core first, overcome the hidden inner blocks holding you back, and then start taking action to change the world around you.

Outer Blocks

Before we go deep into uncovering your hidden inner blocks, it's worth mentioning the outer obstacles you may face on your journey. By definition, outer blocks are external in nature. An example would be economic conditions such as a poor job market. At times, outer blocks could be outside your control. On the other hand, you may be able to take action to overcome others. For instance, another outer block could be that you lack the specific knowledge or training needed to make your next move. Obviously, there is a way to address that particular obstacle with the right strategy and implementation. I don't want to get too deep into outer blocks and how to overcome them at the moment. I will be covering this in more depth throughout the book. The important idea here is that you can't make the necessary changes to your outer game until you have mastered the inner game.

Inner blocks are the dangerous obstacles that really hold you back. The worst case is you may not even realize it. Internally, you allow these inner blocks to zap your energy. When working with clients, I tackle the inner game first—working on that "nut behind the wheel." Many clients call me because they are frustrated and angry at the slow pace of their career advancement. They feel underutilized in their current roles and want to make a bigger impact in their careers. But before we can start developing a vision, strategy, and implementation plan to make changes, we start by addressing the inner blocks in order to clear the path and develop the mindset built for success.

Limiting Beliefs

There are four inner blocks that affect your performance and ability to succeed. The first is limiting beliefs. Limiting beliefs are classified as general beliefs about the world around you, the environment you are in, and the situation or the people around you that you believe are standing in your way. Typically, your limiting beliefs are based on something you learned from someone else or something that happened to you in the past. In fact, these beliefs may even originate from media coverage, movies, or long-standing stereotypes. They are formed through repeated thoughts in your mind, and the reason they hold weight is because you decided they are true.

A few examples of collective limiting beliefs around leadership and career success include: "Successful people are just plain lucky." "Money only comes with hard work." "Leaders are born, not made." "Women can never show emotions when in leadership roles." "Dreams are not practical." What are some of your limiting beliefs that are important for you to challenge so you can move forward?

Once you've identified your limiting beliefs there are ways you can challenge them. How? Explore what effect each limiting belief has had on your life, both negatively and positively. Ask yourself, "Where did I get that idea from?" "How true is that belief, really?" By providing yourself evidence to the contrary, you'll start to slowly let the belief go. Start becoming aware of situations where you are looking for evidence to support your limiting belief. Then, challenge yourself to test the validity of the belief.

Assumptions

The second type of inner block is assumptions. Assumptions are more personal than limiting beliefs. They more intimately involve you and those around you. An assumption is believing that because something happened in the past, it is going to happen again.

Here's a good example of how an assumption will hold you back in your career. Let's say you applied for a promotion at work. You didn't meet all the qualifications, but let's say you met 50 percent of the requirements. You made it through the first round and got the interview, but you were not selected for the promotion. You may *assume* you didn't get the job because you didn't meet 100 percent of the requirements. However, it may simply be that another person was a better fit in the role. If you hold on to the *assumption* that you didn't get the promotion because you only met 50 percent of the qualifications, you might be reluctant to try for another position unless you meet the qualifications 100 percent. Do you see the problem here? Your assumption on why you didn't get the job may not have anything to do with the actual reasoning. In fact, you may later find out that management had another role in mind for you. But if you perpetuate the erroneous assumption, you may never possess the confidence to try again in the future.

The main question to ask yourself when challenging an assumption is simply this: "Just because that happened in the past, why must it happen that way again?" Assumptions are primarily based on personal experiences rather than the outside influences that contribute to formulating limiting beliefs. This is why assumptions can be a bit harder to overcome, but with awareness and coaching, you can move past them.

Interpretations

The third inner block that is holding you back is the barrier built by false interpretations. When you *interpret* something, you're actually creating an opinion about an event, situation, or experience. Most people believe their interpretations are correct when, actually, an interpretation often represents only one perspective among the many that are possible.

Let's go back to the promotion example. A good example of an interpretation may look like this: You *interpret* the fact that the company has never placed a woman in this particular role before to mean that, as a woman, you have no chance for the position. It's your opinion, or *interpretation*, that just because a woman has never been in that role before, it's likely a woman will never be placed in that role in the future. A different perspective may be that a qualified woman has never applied for the position before, and that's why a woman has not been in that role yet.

If you believe your viewpoint of a particular situation is the *only* explanation, you might not be aware of another point of view. You end up wasting a lot of time marching off in the wrong direction, or, in this case, not even applying for a position because of your interpretation of the potential results. If you stick with just your first and only interpretation of a situation like this, you will have little chance of focusing on any other possibility. As a result, you may feel you have no control over what may or can happen next.

Asking yourself one simple question can directly challenge interpretations: "What's another way to look at that?" Again, as with all the inner blocks, it starts with awareness. Once you are aware that you are making an interpretation, you can ask yourself the question to look at the obstacle differently. In some cases, particularly in a corporate environment, it may help you to ask others for their ideas. Asking for another person's perspective on a particular situation may open your eyes to different ways of looking at the same thing. This will challenge your own point of view and help you to break through your individual interpretation.

Inner Critic

The fourth and perhaps the strongest inner block is your inner critic. Think of your inner critic as that micro-managing boss sitting on your shoulder who consistently tells you you're not good enough. It's that voice in your head that expresses criticism, frustration, and even disapproval of your actions. Your inner critic tells you not to even try, never take a risk, always take the easy path, and to limit your career by playing small.

The primary message from your inner critic is that you're just plain not good enough to reach your pinnacle of success. Regardless of any evidence to the contrary, your inner critic's annoying voice continues to whisper to you, "Hey, Babe, it ain't going to happen." It's personal, deeply rooted, and intensely emotional. Push past your inner critic, and you really have broken through your inner glass ceiling.

How many times have you heard that whisper of a voice say: "I don't deserve success and wealth." "Who am I kidding?" "I'm not smart enough to do this job." "What if they find out that I'm a fraud?" "I'll never be able to launch my own business." "I can't possibly change careers at this stage of my life." These are all criticism from your inner critic. Recognize when your inner critic is talking and taking up space in your mind.

What can you do to overcome the strongest of these inner blocks? As with the others, start with increasing your awareness. Many times you don't even realize the inner critic's presence. Catch yourself the next time you are feeling anxious, distracted, or paralyzed. Identify the voice and get personal. Sometimes it helps to give this voice a name and an image. My inner critic is named Dexter, and he looks a lot like the Tasmanian Devil, aka "Taz" from Looney Toons. Whenever Dexter starts chatting, I recognize his voice and can talk firmly and directly to him.

The inner critic's job is to make you feel safe and in control. To counter that, always start by asking yourself, "What am I afraid of? What would it mean if that happened?" Digging deep into the thoughts and emotions behind the fear allows your most vulnerable feelings to rise. It is this vulnerability that your inner critic is trying to protect you from. Do you need all that heavy-duty protection? Probably not. Once you recognize the vulnerability, you can shift your thoughts to quiet your inner critic. Repeatedly empowering yourself by energizing your thoughts in a positive, encouraging manner does wonders to help overcome your inner critic.

Unfortunately, your inner critic will never fully leave your side. After all, he or she does have an important job at times. Bottom line, your inner critic wants you to be safe. Play small. Not to push boundaries. Sometimes, we need that comfort. But when you are trying to make significant and lasting change in your life, your inner critic can hold you back from even trying. Find the balance between comfort and your ability to succeed and become aware of your inner critic's voice. You always have a choice on how to deal with it.

Attitude Adjustment

Your inner glass ceiling is the combination of your inner blocks that prevent you from taking action, claiming your expertise, owning your power, and receiving all that you are worth. This is why I feel this is the most important first step in your career advancement strategy.

Moving through these inner blocks requires commitment and engagement. Your awareness is a choice. Changing your thoughts, beliefs, and perspective is a choice. Once you achieved awareness, shift your focus to your attitude. Attitude is the second A in the Success Factor Mindset Model. Awareness alone won't change your results. Action with the wrong attitude can create unintentional results. So, you must choose how to engage in action with the right success-focused attitude.

Attitude is about your engagement level. The higher your level of engagement, the more positive your attitude and the more likely you will be able to take inspired action. If you are not engaged, you will be unable to make a choice. How can you determine your engagement level? Simply by taking notice of the language you use.

The lowest level of engagement is characterized by "won't." For instance, "I won't write that report" or "I won't take action to change my circumstances." At this stage, there is no energy or effort to get engaged. Things just happen no matter what you think or believe. Refusal is a choice. In this instance, the choice is inaction. There are consequences associated with inaction just as there are results associated with action.

Your attitude at this lowest level of engagement might be defiant. In a corporate setting, the worst-case scenario is the actively disengaged employee. These workers act on their unhappiness and undermine the work their engaged co-workers are trying to accomplish. These folks are easy to spot as they are full of negative energy and refuse to see anything positive in a situation.

As you increase your engagement, your language starts
to change. The next phase is considered a short-term
perspective—"I have to." Here you recognize the need
to complete the task in front of you, but you don't
necessarily see the benefits. Individuals at this level
typically force the situation and exert a tremendous
amount of effort to get through the next step in front
of them hoping to find success. An example: "I have to
complete this report or else I might get fired."

At this level, attitude is still somewhat negative but
there is recognition of responsibility. You know you
have to complete the task, but you are not too excited
about it. This is where the vast majority of corporate
employees sit. Essentially, they are checked out and
just punching the clock.

The third phase is more powerful. The language shifts
to "I need to." You are now aware of choices and seek
to find opportunities. You see the potential for success,
which is why you feel the need to do certain things.
Distractions may take you off course, but you are able
to bring yourself back on track by recognizing your next
steps to success.

Your attitude at this level has shifted from negative
to slightly positive. You are starting to see the
opportunities in the challenges presented to you and
you take more responsibility in taking action. This is the
first level of engagement where your awareness and
attitude can begin to form the right actions for change.

Finally, the highest level of engagement is "I choose to." At this level, you are fully engaged because you feel and believe you have complete choice in the matter. You are completely absorbed in the enjoyment and excitement of what can be. There is a powerful connection between who you are and what you want to do. It is at this level that you are finally able to break through your inner glass ceiling and make choices to build your successful outcomes.

Finding your way to the highest levels of engagement is a process. By first becoming aware of the inner blocks that hold you back, you can consciously choose your thoughts to overcome them. Over time, those thoughts shift your attitude from pessimistic and unconstructive to encouraging and productive. Attitude reflects altitude. With a positive and uplifting attitude, inspired action can take place. Now let's move on to what actions will help you make your best next move.

► FUEL FOR THOUGHT ◄

- The corporate glass ceiling is the invisible barrier that prevents women from reaching high-level leadership positions.

- Your inner glass ceiling is the combination of your inner blocks that prevent you from taking action, claiming your expertise, owning your power, and receiving all that you are worth.

- There are four types of inner blocks: limiting beliefs, assumptions, interpretations, and your inner critic.

- Develop a success mindset with the Success Factor Mindset Model: Awareness—Attitude—Action.

CHAPTER FOUR

Evaluate the Culture

*Company cultures are like country cultures.
Never try to change one. Try, instead, to work
with what you've got.*

PETER F. DRUCKER

In any corporate or workplace environment, organization and culture are vitally important to a high-achieving woman's success. Organization is different from culture. You can have a company with the organization that promotes advancement but a culture contrary to supporting women on that path. On the other hand, a corporate culture may encourage women in leadership, but the organizational structure is difficult to manage. As you move through your career, recognizing and understanding the nuances of organizational structure and culture will help you immensely to choose your best next move.

Organizational Structure

Knowing the structure of an organization is essential to understanding the organization. Hierarchical structures are typically found in large corporate settings. Hierarchies are characterized by a single person or group of people concentrated at the top of the organization. Numerous layers of people support the executive power center. Each individual has clear roles and responsibilities with the level of accountability increasing by each higher layer. This structure tends to be more closed and bureaucratic in nature.

On the other hand, a matrix organizational structure is considered a team approach. Individuals with differing skill sets representing multiple business functions are joined together for a specific task or project. Typically a program manager leads these teams. This structure tends to focus on collaboration and be more open and participative in nature.

Ever see one of those organizational charts with lots of solid and dotted lines? That would be an example of a hybrid structure. The overall organizational structure may be hierarchical, while the support—for instance, in product development—may be matrix to ensure cross-functional participation. These hybrid organizations make it a bit more difficult to manage your career path, which is why many refer to the corporate jungle gym rather than the corporate ladder.

It's important you understand how an organization is structured because understanding will help you identify the key influencers and foreshadow potential obstacles you may encounter on your career advancement journey. Obstacles appear at every corner of your path. Some are easier to navigate than others. The structure of the organization will show you the best methods to overcome these obstacles. However, structure alone will not determine your success in overcoming these obstacles.

Culture

Aileron, a national non-profit organization dedicated to unleashing the potential of private businesses through professional management, defines culture as the "values and beliefs as demonstrated through the *real* behavior of the organization." This definition captures the heart of the issue. An organization can have stated values and beliefs that define their culture. However, it is only through the real behaviors and how the organization lives up to those stated values that determine the true culture. Furthermore, what is *allowed* to happen is actually *promoted* by leadership. This is why it is important to observe a culture in action and not just rely on the defined values listed on a company's website.

Throughout my career I have seen and been a part of cultural change management teams. Leadership may say they want a culture to change, but unless they walk the talk, change does not occur. For example, in one large corporation I worked at, there was an attempt to radically change the culture within the organization to encourage input from all levels. Although the message was to "raise your hand" and "speak up with concerns," the prevailing culture was still "shoot the messenger if the news isn't what you want to hear." As a result, employees were still shy to bring up problems and issues to senior leaders for fear of retribution.

In my experience, the culture of an organization is the critical piece to decipher in order to truly understand one's potential for success. As a woman in a male-dominated discipline or industry, I learned the culture of the organization will tell you more about a woman's prospective success than anything else.

If the culture does not support the advancement of women, you have two choices. Either you can decide you will be the trailblazer or you can decide that your efforts will be best rewarded in another environment. For high-achieving women, this decision may be a difficult one to make.

Industry Cultures

My first full-time position after graduation from Purdue was in Auburn Hills, Michigan, working for Chrysler Corporation. After spending three summers as an engineering intern with Chrysler at multiple locations, I had a good sense of the company and the opportunities for advancement. I was placed in their competitive Chrysler Institute of Engineering (CIE) program for the first two years. During that time, I rotated through six different parts of the business while working toward my master's degree in mechanical engineering in the evenings. The CIE was a fantastic program that allowed me to learn more about the parts of the business I was most interested in while gaining exposure throughout the company.

However, I also learned a great deal about the culture during my rotations. Keen observation and conversation with other CIE graduates taught me a few important things. Even though as a CIE I was tagged as high potential, the path of advancement once I graduated was unclear.

Many CIEs were struggling in their mid-careers, trying to break into a management position. They saw immediate advancement early in their careers, but then their careers stalled. Observing their experiences, I realized that the fast track into management had essentially two paths.

The first path was defined by the culture of the automotive industry. Generations of families worked in the industry, resulting in nepotism throughout the ranks. If a person had an automotive bloodline, they were more likely to get advancement opportunities. Senior leaders were always looking out for family members. Employees who were tagged as high potential but did not have the automotive bloodline demonstrated the second path. The key to their success was to leave the corporate environment, go work at a supplier for a few years, increase their business and technical knowledge, influence, network, and then re-enter the corporate organization at the management level.

This was the early 1990s. Generations before had been rewarded for loyalty to the company with pensions, advancement, and security. But the industry was changing. Those securities and expectations were shifting. Once I recognized that staying at Chrysler would be a long, slow advancement process since I didn't have the automotive bloodline, I realized I had to take action to leave. At that point, I made the conscious choice to seek new opportunities and pursue my passion in professional motorsports. Ironically, my theories were later proven when I rejoined the corporate world twenty years later in the commercial trucking industry. I entered Navistar at the management level and saw numerous employees with ten to fifteen years of experience, and no familial bloodline into leadership at the company, struggling to advance into management positions.

Another example of culture differences occurred when I first entered the motorsports industry at Honda. My initial role was operations manager responsible for logistics and business contracts with the race teams.

The racing industry had the stereotypical view that women at the racetrack were only involved in public relations or marketing (or were the girlfriends of the drivers). No one believed I had a technical background, let alone more education and degrees than the vast majority of engineers at the track. As I attempted to get more involved in technical matters at Honda, I fought internal pushback. Even though I was more than capable of handling the daily engineering tasks, I was continually denied the opportunity to participate. I eventually came to the realization that the only way I would gain the respect as a technical contributor in the industry was to actually go and be an engineer. My prospects for advancement into executive management were limited until I proved myself.

I was at a crossroad. It became apparent that pursuing a technical role within Honda would be blocked and fought every step of the way by the American management. There were several senior managers that were happy to keep me in an operational and logistics role with no input on the technical matters. In fact, my own boss kept trying to block all opportunities to contribute technically. The difficulty was that there were also a number of Japanese senior leaders that were supportive of where I wanted to go. I faced a difficult decision. Do I stay or do I go?

Early in your career you will come across these types of obstacles that make you stop for a moment and consider the alternatives. But before you just go job-hopping, hopeful to find a way through the obstacle somewhere else, it's vitally important you first try to break through where you are. If all you do is keep moving to new companies expecting things to be radically different, you will be in for a big disappointment.

You have to honestly try to work within the organization before you deem it unworthy of your additional Herculean efforts to succeed. Otherwise, you will just end up making the same mistakes over and over again never learning how to manage around obstacles. It's all about being persistent—to a point.

This time you take is critically important to framing your best next move. Now is the time to evaluate the organization and the culture you are facing. What is the likelihood for your success? Can you be a trailblazer and break through? Or will you be constantly banging your head against the proverbial brick wall with no hope of ever busting through to the other side? You'll want to seriously consider these questions and you can start by understanding how you think.

What Type of Thinker Are You?

With over twenty years of experience in start-up organizations, small niche businesses, consulting firms, and multi-national corporations spanning multiple industries, I have determined there are two types of thinkers, which I cover in the following paragraphs. Knowing which type of thinker you are will help you greatly in finding the right organization and culture for you to thrive.

First, there is the process thinker. Most of your conversations are about the process. "We have done this. We are doing that. Finally we will arrive at this point." If you're embedded in this type of thinking, you tend to rely on what has worked in the past. There are exceptions. You can still be a process thinker with new ideas on how to change a process, but if the environment you are in is resistant to change, you will end up frustrated.

Process thinkers congregate successfully in corporate organizations. The corporate mindset is built around process. Manufacturing process, engineering design process, development process, sales process, and delivery process are just some examples. If you are a process thinker, you will excel in the corporate environment.

The second type of thinker is the instinctive thinker. Instincts, or gut feel, drive the decision-making process. These thinkers may still review data and look at the process, but the primary motivator to making a decision is based on instinct. For the most part, these people see the bigger picture and have a sense of the overall impact a decision will have on a situation.

Because of their nature, instinctive thinkers tend to launch new endeavors, propose radical new ideas, and lead from a visionary perspective. Their style embraces an entrepreneurial mindset. To succeed, the culture in which they work must encourage out-of-the-box thinking and reward decisions based on their intuition.

Diversity and Inclusion

Embedded mindsets are often institutional as well as individual. Unfortunately, these mindsets are a reality in Corporate America and difficult to eradicate. A CEO's personal mission to change behavior does not reach all levels. Targeting behavioral change generally leads only to an early burst of accomplishment followed by a setback to old ways. A diversity program by itself, no matter how comprehensive, is no match for well-established beliefs.

Believe it or not, there are still managers (men *and* women) who believe women cannot succeed in particular roles. For instance, the path to senior management for women may only be in the traditionally female path of human-resource management rather than the male-dominated areas of finance or engineering. Even worse, managers make assumptions about women without even asking for their input. An example—a hiring manager assumes a woman would not want a position because of the increase in travel and the effects it would have on her family.

The Society of Human Resource Management (SHRM) defines diversity as "the collective mixture of differences and similarities that include, for example, individual and organizational characteristics, values, beliefs, experiences, backgrounds, preferences, and behaviors." Inclusion, while related, is a separate concept. SHRM defines inclusion as "the achievement of a work environment in which all individuals are treated fairly and respectfully, have equal access to opportunities and resources, and can contribute fully to the organization's success."

The problem lies in the organization that has one but not the other. It must have both diversity and inclusion. Diversity has long been a business objective as a matter of compliance. In that aspect, companies are fulfilling the requirements for diversity. Research shows in an increasingly competitive economy where talent is crucial to the bottom line, diversity produces a more creative, innovative, and productive workforce. Therefore, it is imperative for an organization to promote a diverse workforce.

Inclusion, on the other hand, is different. You can have a diverse workforce that drives economic growth, but if these employees are not included throughout the ranks of the organization, that diversity will eventually disappear. Inclusion promotes engagement. By actively including the diverse workforce in the opportunities to contribute and lead, a company's bottom line will dramatically increase in relation to the engagement level of their employees.

Evaluating the Culture

So, how do you evaluate the culture of a company? How do you know if your persistence will pay off? Or when is it time to pack your bags and seek new adventures?

Ask yourself these questions:

1. How many women serve on the board of directors? How many women are represented in senior leadership (C-Suite and senior executive staff)?

2. What is the senior leadership commitment to advance women at all levels of the organization?

3. What networks are available or unavailable to women? What informal networks meet to actively discourage or encourage women?

4. What leadership-development-plan process for individuals does the organization have? How well are women represented in the process? Are women proportionately represented?

5. What measurement of results to show achievement of more women in higher-level positions does the organization use?

6. What is the perception of fairness amongst all employees—men and women, regardless of position?

7. What evidence is there that the right people are being promoted for the right reasons?

8. How well are senior-level men sponsoring women?

9. How open and comfortable do leaders appear discussing the aspirations of women and asking about them?

10. How do women in the organization feel in terms of belonging and being treated equally?

Finding the right organization and culture to thrive in is a personal endeavor. What work for some may not work for others. You have to be able to fit within the structure and character of a company to perform at your best. Find a corporate culture with men that have a strong desire to support and advance women. Culture is driven from the top down. Leadership defines the values, and more importantly, the behaviors of a culture and organization. These values show up significantly in overall decision-making and how to promote from within.

As a woman, you first have to figure out what you want. Start with perfecting your inner game. Get clear and focused on your own strengths, values, priorities, and goals. Then, evaluate your organization and culture. You always have choices.

Reach out to others (both men and women) in your organization to truly understand the culture. If your career goal is to pursue an executive role, it's imperative you find the right industry, organization, and culture to support your path. Discuss the expectations—both your own and your organization's—of the executive role you are pursuing. Do they match your personal values, priorities, talents, and strengths? You are the driver in this race. You make the moves to open new doors of opportunity.

Now back to that crossroad in my racing career. After consideration and reflection, I knew it was time to walk away and pursue a technical role elsewhere in the industry. Once I made my decision, I mentioned my desire within my personal network. Within a few weeks, Ilmor Engineering, one of Honda's competitors, heard I was seeking an engineering position. Ilmor knew of my strong work ethic, competitive nature, and results-driven attitude through business interactions within the race series. The company was adding teams and needed additional engineers to provide trackside support. As a result, I joined Ilmor and became the first female engine engineer in IndyCar racing. I reached a new level of success and opportunity because I made the decision to find a company culture to support my goals. The added benefits: amazing worldwide media attention and a new trajectory for my career.

▶ FUEL FOR THOUGHT ◀

- Organizational structure and culture are key ingredients in your potential success.

- Culture is defined as the "values and beliefs as demonstrated through the *real* behaviors of the organization."

- Process thinkers embrace the corporate mindset. Instinctive thinkers embody an entrepreneurial mindset.

- Diversity and inclusion are two separate concepts that are related. You must have both to succeed.

CHAPTER FIVE

How to Join the Club without Becoming a Man

To be nobody by myself—in a world doing its best, night and day, to make me somebody else— means to fight the hardest battle any human can fight, and never stop fighting.

E.E. CUMMINGS

Besides an organizational culture not supportive of women, there is another obstacle to overcome— The Good Ol' Boys' Club. The Good Ol' Boys' Club is an informal and extremely powerful network of primarily men who support, recommend, defend, and promote one another. In the business world, this club, or inner circle, is where the behind-the-scenes activity takes place. Business deals are developed, new client opportunities shared, advancement strategies defined. By sticking together, these comrades share precious information only revealed to those in the club. Women *have* joined the club and I will tell you how you can too.

As part of the club, a male protégé gets access and opportunity based on his potential to deliver results. Unfortunately, women don't get this access. Since most of senior leadership in business is still predominately men, they are comfortable promoting men based on how they think they will perform in a role but are uncomfortable doing the same for women. Instead, the men want demonstrated accomplishments from women—basically, facts and proof that she would succeed in a role before offering her the opportunity.

Women know this is reality in the corporate world. How many times have you seen one of your male co-workers get promoted to a new position even though he lacks the requisite experience? Heck, he may even have screwed up more things than he did right! How does it happen that he's still promoted? It's all part of his being a member in the club.

The club is a political organization. Members know how to navigate the politics of their organization and industry. Senior members mentor new recruits to the way of doing business. Potential new members must meet stringent membership qualifications to be admitted. Unfortunately, in most cases, those qualifications require a specific gender (male). Those who desire a position in senior leadership discover it's important to understand the inner workings of the club and how to become a member even if gender challenged (female).

Back in the 1980s, as women began to take on more traditional roles in the business world, women were taught that in order to join this exclusive club, they had to act like a man. Advice ranged from dressing more like a man to posturing and yelling in meetings. The fashion was big shoulder pads, pinstriped suits, white blouses with floppy little ties. Make-up was discouraged. Women didn't want to confuse the poor men by showing sexuality while at work. Bright colors, and especially pastels, were discouraged. Stick with the black and navy blue suit with a crispy, white button-down shirt underneath.

Once women got the uniform right, they had to think and act like a man. Be more aggressive in meetings. Raise their voices and lower the pitch. Show their anger by banging their fists on the table, but absolutely never let men see them cry. Be dominant and bullish. Work hard and put in longer hours than their coworkers. Make sure they are the first to arrive and the last to leave the office. And especially for women—go way above and beyond their job descriptions. If women managed to handle all that, they just *might* see the door to the club open slightly.

Oh, how the times have changed. Let's speed ahead to the new millennium.

The club still exists; however, the process to join has evolved. No longer is it about looking like and acting like a man. The best opportunities for career advancement still remain within these informal networks. The secret to your career success is to join the club *without* becoming a man.

So, just what does it take?

▶ **First and foremost, you must gain respect for the knowledge and contributions you bring to the team.** Leverage your unique strengths and talents. Be seen and recognized as a competent contributor. Make the men take notice of your great ideas, your fresh perspective, your logical thinking, and your accurate preparation. By gaining their respect before trying to join the club, you can make opening that door a little bit easier.

▶ **You must promote yourself and your accomplishments.** If you don't take credit for your work, who will? Unfortunately I have seen clients resist taking credit for their contributions time and time again. The result is women, who have worked hard and succeeded delivering projects on time and under budget, continually passed over for promotion. They came from a time where hard work was recognized and honored.

That's not the case now. If you don't step up to promote yourself and your work, no one will notice you. Again, it's back to the speed of business. Technological advancements have forced the focus on the next best thing instantaneously. No one has time to review and recognize individual participation. It's up to you to create a personal brand with impact and a strong presence. Your brand communicates your strengths and accomplishments when you are not physically there to promote yourself.

▶ **Your communication style needs to be clear, concise, and confident.** That means no rambling. Just get to the point. You know what I'm talking about. Women have a tendency to ramble. When men hear rambling, they immediately switch off their brain. It's like Charlie Brown's teacher talking to them. It doesn't matter how great the idea is, if you rattle on and on with too much detail, your idea will go unnoticed. Listen first. Ask specific questions. Compose your idea, and *then* add to the conversation with impact. Less is more. Try it. You'll see what I mean.

Also, make sure you speak using confident language. One of my biggest peeves is to hear women continually saying they are sorry. Stop saying it! If you made a mistake, own the mistake. Stop apologizing all the time. Acknowledge your error, then go back and fix it. When presenting your ideas, be confident. Don't use phrases like "I think," "I'm not really sure," or "Would it be okay?" Use strong language to portray confidence and back your message up with powerful body language. Sit tall. Take up space at the conference table. Don't be afraid to push back on an idea you disagree with, particularly in a group setting. Just keep your response succinct and to the point.

▶ **You must be more strategic in your thinking.**
There are short-term and long-term goals in your career advancement. In order to be able to accomplish any of your goals, you must develop the right alliances and networks, both internally and externally. Men and women typically work to develop their internal network when initially joining a company. You need to connect with those go-to people who can help you navigate the system as you learn the ropes.

But equally as important is continuing to develop your external network. Women especially need to look beyond the walls of their current company to develop relationships with others in their industry and beyond. This is where the club excels and how men can easily move between companies and into higher leadership positions. Get out there and make connections. Reach out to others to understand their perspectives. Ask questions and learn. Start to see the bigger picture of how you can fit in and contribute.

Business gets done through relationships. Find out how you can help others succeed and move forward before expecting anything in return. Offer to be a connector by bringing ideas and people together focused on a common goal. Give freely of your expertise, knowledge, and skills. It's like building up favors. You know how this works, but you may not realize the significance within the club.

Now before you go crazy giving and giving (which I know women have a wonderful tendency to overdo), you must develop the skill to ask for help in return. This is the hidden gem of success within the club. Sure, everyone appreciates help and support for their own activities. After making significant contributions, it is your turn to ask for support to make your next move. You will gain more respect with the right supporters by asking for their input, advice, and receiving their support than you will by only giving. Remember, it's a two-way street out there. Make sure you ask for and receive what you need to move forward.

▶ **Hang out with the right crowd.** Women tend to socialize and spend most of their time with peers or direct reports and, most notably, other women. Men spend more of their time managing up in an organization. Sure, it might be outside your comfort zone to be spending more time with senior-level people, but it's the only way to get the perspective of leadership and to be able to incorporate that perspective into your strategic thinking. Spend time with those in positions higher than your current rank. Be inquisitive and ask questions about their challenges. By gaining insight to what they're facing you may be able to come in with a fresh perspective and new ideas that can help solve some of the issues they can't see for themselves. This will go a long way towards getting that advancement door open for you.

▶ **Be assertive but not aggressive.** This is a slight shift from the 1980s to today. Think of assertive as aggressive with a feminine twist. It is not about being bossy (a term most women are certainly afraid of these days). Assertive is about how women handle themselves in certain circumstances. Knowing when to turn on and off their more forceful masculine traits is crucial to be successful.

In a 2011 study at the Stanford Graduate School of Business, women who were able to self-monitor their behavior were very successful professionally. "These women were able to be chameleons, to fit into their environment by assessing social situations and adapting their actions appropriately," explains Dr. Olivia O'Neill, coauthor of the study. These women received one-and-a-half times more promotions than masculine men, and received three times as many promotions as masculine women who did not self-monitor.

A chameleon? What a *great* analogy of how to fit into the club without becoming a man.

▶ **Don't make things personal.** Ever notice how men can get into a heated argument and an hour later head off to lunch together like nothing ever happened? It's because men don't take things personally. They can get angry and lash out at one another to get their point across, but then be able to shrug it off as part of doing business. Women have a tendency to take everything personally or as a personal attack.

With a little practice, you can stop personalizing things. When you stop being so critical of yourself, you too can have the important conversations, allow the tempers to flare, and then let things go.

It's still not a good idea to let others see you cry. You do have to keep your cool and control your emotions. However, there are times where the softer side of you can come through and it's okay. But don't allow your emotions to control you. Compassion is one thing. Overwhelming emotions are another.

▶ **Find a way to join in the informal conversations.** Casual conversation is where business gets done, opportunities are created, and leaders are made. Club members are part of the coveted information loop. Those outside the club are not privy to the information. It is critical that you find a way to access that information; to make strides and continually move forward, you must find a way to join in these casual conversations.

First find out where these conversations are taking place. Perhaps the guys get together for a cup of coffee at Starbucks first thing in the morning. Maybe they go out for drinks at the local watering hole right after work. Don't forget the golf course. You need to observe where and how these informal conversations are taking place and then figure out the best way to get yourself included.

Now, I realize you may have concerns about going out after work with the guys for a couple of drinks. It's normal to worry about the stigma you as a woman having cocktails with a group of men may have on your overall reputation. However, you should not let the potential of becoming the wrong kind of F.A.S.T. Woman stop you in your pursuit of joining this important informal network. If you're worried about your overall image and reputation, then set a time limit and leave before it gets too late. For example, if you know the group typically goes out for drinks and dinner, make sure you leave by 10 pm. When traveling for business, having a strict end time is of utmost importance. A female executive in the commercial trucking industry once told me, "Nothing good happens after 10 pm." Good observation. Set your boundaries and monitor yourself so nothing bad can happen.

Getting into the informal conversation is critical to successfully joining the club. When I first joined Navistar's Engine Group, we had an off-site, two-day leadership conference. After dinner, a group of male managers meandered over to the bar for a few cocktails. I took this opportunity to join them so I could get to know them better on a personal level. It proved to be very beneficial. Yes, I was back in my room before 10 pm. But the informal time with a few key leaders proved to be essential later in my career.

One of those guys I kicked back a few drinks with eventually became our vice president of engine engineering. Because of the informal relationship we started and continued, I had developed rapport and respect on a personal as well as professional level. During controversial times, I was able to sit at the table of senior leadership, present a differing opinion, and be heard with respect. Although the VP disagreed with my position (and had no difficulty making that well known in a meeting with the corporate senior management), my perspective was heard, and I was later promoted to oversee the new product implementation. My success was due in part to developing personal and professional relationships to enable my membership in the club while not taking anything personally.

▶ **You must be able to handle some humor and teasing.** Guys are often part of good-natured banter. They tease and kid around with one another at times. When you, as a woman, are included in this day-to-day banter, it's a sign you're considered as part of the group or as one of the guys. Being able to tease you and include you in their banter means they're comfortable and accepting of having you around. But there are limits.

By no means am I suggesting you have no filters or boundaries to the humor and teasing. Sexual harassment is real and should never be overlooked. Women in male-dominated disciplines and industries do need to have a bit thicker skin in order to succeed.

Determine your own comfort level with humor and teasing. When someone comes close to your limit, or crosses it, make sure you let him know that he has crossed the line. Unless you communicate, with respect, the other party won't know where that line is for you.

Believe me, someone will cross your line no matter how high you place it. When it happens, point it out, explain why you felt disrespected, and request that it doesn't happen again. More than likely, you will not have to deal with that uncomfortable situation again. You will gain the respect of the men you work with. If it happens continuously after you have addressed the culprit, then it is time to notify human resources and pursue a more formal cease-and-desist arrangement.

▶ **Finally, the most important secret to joining the club without becoming a man is to be authentic.** Authenticity drives confidence. It allows others to see you at your best. Your performance soars, and people take notice. Being authentic is about developing your personal brand to encompass your strengths, talents, experiences, knowledge, and perspective at the highest level. Men notice women who are authentic. At work, they want to support, sponsor, and engage with you. There are no hidden agendas at play. The team, and the club, accepts you just as you are. You are your most powerful self when you are your *authentic* self. Learn to stand in your power.

Believe it or not, men know when you are pretending or if you are trying too hard to fit in. If you are overly sensitive and take things too personally, they know it. Be confident in your own skin. Be yourself. Not only are authenticity and confidence attractive traits, they will lower barriers and open doors. Once you are seen naturally as a team player, you're in the club.

▶ FUEL FOR THOUGHT ◀

- The Good Ol' Boys' Club (a.k.a. the club) is an informal and extremely powerful network of primarily men who support, recommend, defend, and promote one another.

- The secret to your career success is to join the club *without* becoming a man.

- Gain respect for the knowledge, strengths, and skills you bring to the team.

- Promote yourself and your accomplishments with a strong personal brand.

- Be clear, concise, and confident in your communication.

- Find a way to join the informal conversations and networks.

- Be authentic.

CHAPTER SIX

Take More Career Risks

You will either step forward into growth, or you will step back into safety.

ABRAHAM MASLOW

What are the three biggest risks you have taken professionally in the past twelve months? Think about it. Can you come up with three? How about just one? If you are like most career women, you are struggling to come up with an answer. Taking risks in your career is the best method to advance in leadership, increase your income, and create endless opportunities.

Risk is defined as uncertainty, variability of return, the possibility of suffering loss, vulnerability. Individuals interpret the degree and type of risk differently. For instance, one woman may feel that speaking up with an opposing viewpoint in a senior leadership meeting might be risky. Another may consider the idea of accepting a global assignment uncertain for her personal and professional life. Yet another woman may feel risk is leaving the perceived security of a corporate job to take the leap into entrepreneurship. However one defines risk, the point is that women need to take more of them.

Catalyst, the leading nonprofit organization dedicated to expanding opportunities for women in business, reported that 40 percent of women in leadership positions say that going after difficult and visible assignments was the key to their career advancement. Taking on these types of assignments carries a degree of risk. There are no guarantees for success. Even with the uncertainty, taking calculated risks in one's career is vital for several important reasons.

Pushing Past Your Career Comfort Zone

The first year at a new company is exciting. You are meeting new people, learning new things, and figuring out how to get things done. After a while, you start to settle in. A few years go by and you know exactly who to go to and how to get around any obstacles to accomplish your tasks. There is a sense of familiarity in your work. You know the people, the process, and the product. Your workdays become routine. You begin to fall into the work trap where you feign being busy to avoid doing new things. Productivity starts to drop. You have lost the drive and ambition to do more or learn new things.

People like to be comfortable. They enjoy the familiar and routine. Even when the familiar is horrible, people will resist change. Although a work environment may be frustrating and stressful, employees know what to expect and how to handle it. They don't bother trying to change or try something new, because it could be worse than what they already have. Stick with the devil you know rather than risk trying something new.

Seeking comfort, however natural it feels, will never enable professional (or personal) growth. No one achieves greatness by playing it safe. By not pushing yourself to expand beyond your comfort zone, you have built a false sense of security within your cubicle walls. Complacency is dangerous. If you are not taking risks by pushing the limits of your career comfort zone, you are not fully utilizing the capacity of your full potential. Consider taking bold moves such as a new role in a different functional area, proposing a new idea to senior leadership, or pursuing an international assignment. Try anything that feels out of the ordinary.

Unfortunately, women tend to over estimate the risk itself and under estimate the extent of the opportunity. It's natural to focus on the potential negative consequences of all the things that might go wrong if they take on a new opportunity.

You have likely been conditioned to think this way, which is why it is important to become aware of the limiting beliefs and assumptions that cloud your perspective. Recognize when hidden fears start to come up so you can consciously choose how to respond and take appropriate action. Look beyond the immediate risk to see what the future opportunity may hold. You can begin by asking questions regarding how this opportunity will build your network, increase your influence, or allow you to learn new skills. Make sure you understand the full extent of the opportunity before making a decision.

At the same time, you must also evaluate the risk of *not* taking action. When you don't take risks in your career, nothing changes. When nothing changes, you end up feeling frustrated and stuck. Staying in your comfort zone may feel more comfortable at the moment, but you open yourself up to risk beyond your control. You never know what could arise. What if you are laid off in company downsizing or are moved to a less-satisfying job or department? Not taking risks keeps you playing small and not living up to your fullest potential.

By pushing past the boundaries of your career comfort zone, you open up the opportunity to create your own destiny by getting out of your own way. Each time you break through an old barrier, your confidence grows. As you expand your thinking, your fears diminish, so the next time you find yourself up against your comfort-zone boundaries, it isn't quite as scary. Risk-taking becomes easier the more you do it.

Opportunities Arise from Risk

Risk can be viewed negatively or positively. Reframing the idea of risk can directly impact results. Many successful women leaders simply reframe risk as an opportunity to *succeed* rather than a path to failure. Sandra Peterson, CEO of the $10 billion business Bayer CropScience, told *Forbes* in 2011:

"Most women I know who have been successful in business, it's because they've been willing to take on the risky challenge that other people would say, 'Oh, I'm not sure I want to do that.' If you look at my career, I've taken a lot of risky roles. They were risky to some people, but to me it was, 'Wow, this is a great opportunity and it's allowing me to learn new things and take on a bigger role and a bigger organization.' But some people would view that as, 'Are you crazy? What do you know about diabetes, or what do you know about washing machines or the food industry or automobiles or the agricultural industry?'"

Risk-taking over the course of a career is an iterative process. Some risks work out great, others not so much. Either way, the successful woman views risk-taking as a learning experience.

Think about the development of a new product for the marketplace. Engineers start with a design based on the perceived needs of the intended customer. Once an initial design is complete, the product is passed on to the development team. In the development process, engineers test the product for failure. Based on the type and extent of the failure, adjustments are made to the original design to improve performance. This iterative process continues gathering critical information used to make decisions to resolve issues until the product meets and exceeds the expectations for use by the customer.

You career path can be viewed in a similar way. Your career is a long-term product of your strengths, talents, contributions, and knowledge. Career advancement is a process of trial and error. Throughout your development, you will accept some risks that provide instant payoff and others that fail miserably. What is most important is the fact that even if a risk doesn't pay off in the way you expected, you will still learn and grow in the process—and that counts as pay-off too. A new role may not be a good fit for your strengths, but you have a new network of experts to support you in the future. Changing industries might be exactly what you need to challenge yourself and achieve greater rewards. No matter what, continual growth and learning will result from taking more risks.

Remain Nimble in the Era of Change

The only constant in life is change. By staying in your comfort zone, you risk being downsized or obsolete. The speed of technology, access to information, globalization, economic shifts, and political ramifications all impact industry and eventually your career. Taking risks allows you to remain nimble in the face of an ever-changing environment. It is up to you to own your career. Industry will not pave the path for you.

In an ever-changing world, minimizing risk is one of the riskiest things you can do. Pursue intelligent and calculated risks. These are the risks where the potential downside is somewhat limited, but the potential upside is practically unlimited. Those are the risks to jump at. Maintain a sense of urgency regarding your career development. This will keep you moving toward new opportunities for growth and advancement rather than shying away from them. Be curious, confident, and open to new learning.

Breakout opportunities are everywhere you look, but are you ready for them? If it were only a matter of tapping into your network and being resourceful, everyone would enjoy breakthroughs. The reality is resourcefulness is hardly enough when the landscape is continually changing. Risk, just like business and life, is dynamic. You change, the world changes, the competition changes. As you get more comfortable with risk-taking, you remain nimble to adjust and take advantage of change when it comes your way.

One of My Risky Career Moves

Sir Stirling Moss, arguably the greatest all-around racing driver in history and icon of the motorsports world, knew something about risk and reward. Out of the 375 competitive races Moss finished during his professional career, he won an astonishing 212. All of those wins came from taking the challenging route, not avoiding it for comfort. Moss famously said, "To achieve anything in this game you must be prepared to dabble in the boundary of disaster."

The same can be said for spectacular results in your career. How many times have you been richly rewarded for taking the safe and easy path? My guess is not many. Wildly successful women are comfortable with risk. They embrace the challenge and uncertainty that comes with it. For F.A.S.T. Women in Business, risk-taking is a way of life.

After six seasons orchestrating moves within IndyCar racing's Good Ol' Boys' Network, I knew it was time for me to move on. I grew tired of living out of my suitcase, heading to the track at 5 am, and working weekends all summer. The technical challenge of tuning competitive race engines was slowly fading because the economics of the racing industry was changing. Several of the engine manufacturers were departing, leaving only one engine in the series. For a competitive person like me, taking away the competition meant my role was changing. Instead of the challenge of tuning an engine for a driver to gain a tenth of a second on the track, my role would be regulated to just making sure the engine started and finished the race.

I craved something new and challenging. At that point, I realized that throughout my engineering education, I wasn't able to take the business courses I wanted. Before getting into racing, I had thought about getting my MBA, but once the opportunity came in motorsports, I put that idea on the back burner. Now seemed to be the right the time to bring it up to the front. So, I decided to take a calculated risk—walk away from my lucrative job in racing and head back to the classroom full-time.

Planning this risk began nine months before the actual event. I investigated schools, took entrance exams, completed applications, sought out scholarships, saved money for tuition and expenses, and arranged to borrow any remainder I had not saved. There was no guarantee that I would have a job, let alone a better one, when I finished school. Sure, it's scary walking away from what I knew and the comforts of perceived security. But deep down inside, I knew I was headed in the right direction. I had to take this risk, and I trusted that it would pay off in the long run.

With the strategy in place, I took the risk. The road was a bit bumpy, but I thoroughly enjoyed the new direction

I was headed in. Did the road look like I had planned? In some ways, yes. In other ways, no. But in the end, I trusted my inner compass. By continually remaining positive and focused on *success*, new opportunities arose I hadn't expected. I ended up wildly succeeding in ways I hadn't even imagined, all because I took a calculated risk.

The road to your ultimate goal—whether that is a promotion, career change, or entrepreneurship—will be filled with unexpected twists and turns. It's important to stay focused on your intention and remain open to all the possibilities. Continue to get comfortable with taking risks—the small ones and the big ones. The rewards are there for your taking.

There is a Buddhist saying: "If you want to know your past, look into your present *conditions*. If you want to know your future, look into your present *actions*." Risk-taking is all about action. Your career depends on the actions you take today to create opportunities in the future. Investigate the positive risks. Map out a strategy and action plan so you can pave the path to success. By first doing the work to map out a calculated risk, you will greatly increase your probability for success and reduce your anxiety when it's time to act.

▶ FUEL FOR THOUGHT ◀

- Taking calculated risks throughout your career is critical for success.

- Women tend to overestimate the risk itself and underestimate the extent of the opportunity.

- Successful women leaders simply reframe risk as an opportunity to *succeed* rather than a path to fail.

- Taking risks allows you to remain nimble in the face of an ever-changing environment.

- Be curious, confident, and open to new learning.

- Risk-taking is all about taking action.

CHAPTER SEVEN

Play to Your Strengths and Reinvent Yourself

Character cannot be developed in ease and quiet. Only through experience of trial and suffering can the soul be strengthened, ambition inspired, and success achieved.

HELEN KELLER

L ike many people, you may have spent years—or worse, the better part of your life—working on your weaknesses. Remember back in grade school? Teachers were most concerned about those subjects you struggled with rather than the ones you excelled in. As you entered the workforce, this concept was reinforced. Today, in performance reviews, managers barely mention what you are great at and spend the majority of your review discussing those developmental areas for improvement.

Business culture has long focused on weaknesses. Managers and leaders spend massive amounts of time and energy trying to address deficits in themselves and their employees. This focus on weakness eventually becomes a quest to bridge the gaps where one doesn't have any natural capability or talent. In extreme cases, managers attempt to make people into someone they are not.

I'm here to tell you that checking off the boxes to satisfy criteria developed by someone who doesn't necessarily have your best interests in mind in order to overcome your perceived weaknesses is a *big* waste of your time and energy. First of all, this fixing mentality tells you that you cannot move forward until you fix, then cross that item off your list. The fact is you will never completely cross that item off your list. Everyone has blind spots, skills that don't come quite as easily as others. Setting out to eliminate your weaknesses is a losing strategy.

Research suggests that highly successful people start with a dominant talent and then add skills, knowledge, and practice (application). In other words, you stand a greater chance of success if you build on your authentic self—who you already are—beginning with your innate strengths. Unfortunately, you are not conditioned or trained to recognize strengths in yourself. It takes some work and a change in perspective for it to become second nature.

I'm not advising you to turn a blind eye to shortcomings that could potentially derail you in your career. Avoiding critical deficiencies, and the corresponding development work, can only lead to bigger problems for you down the road. Career success is a matter of balance and focus.

Working hard on your weaknesses will never make you excel in your weak areas, but investing in your strengths will bring *exponential* growth and wealth. Everyone has strengths, and when identified, nurtured, and channeled appropriately, they can have a dramatic effect on your job satisfaction and financial success. Your particular strengths form the solid foundation for your massive action campaign— how to reinvent yourself. There are three options when deciding on your best next move to fall in love with Monday mornings again.

Bold Move Option #1: New Position in Your Current Organization or Industry

This option is for you if your company culture supports your advancement and you have managed to join the club. Bold moves within an organization or industry are rarely rewarded with a direct upward climb. You can still move up, but you will likely also move over in the process.

Look for new opportunities outside of your current path. Perhaps it's a move to another department that focuses on another key process. For instance, under the functional area of finance, move from accounting into mergers and acquisitions to get a different perspective on the business. Don't forget the prep work you just did. Only pursue opportunities that play to your strengths. If you are more of a detailed-oriented person, make sure the roles and responsibilities allow you to focus primarily on the details, regardless of the opportunity. You want to keep placing your best foot forward. Taking new positions that allow you to perform at your best means only seeking opportunities that inherently match your strengths.

A bold move might also mean moving to a completely different functional area to increase visibility and add experience supportive of your strengths. A good example is the engineer who wants to have more customer interaction. Transitioning from engineering into marketing or sales might be a smooth move. Of course, I'm assuming this engineer has great communication skills in order to effectively work with customers. Again, focus on strengths to propel you into new arenas.

The key to make this type of move successful is to concentrate on clear communication of your personal brand focused on your unique strengths.

Self-promotion is the ability to communicate your talents, strengths, and accomplishments into a dialogue that also directs people where you want to go. Just recounting tasks and projects that you've completed isn't going to be enough. You must be able to add flavor to your accomplishments in order to project the potential you bring to new opportunities. The juicy flavor you add comes from positioning your strengths as assets. By fine-tuning your language on how you contribute to the organization and highlighting your strengths, you will automatically put your best self forward and project yourself into areas you may not have thought possible.

Taking a new position is also your chance to leverage your club membership. Reach out to your internal network and seek their advice. Particularly when you are seeking to move to a new functional area, these relationships can be extremely helpful. Political connections within the club can get you the introductions you need to pave the path for your best next move.

It is important to understand and recognize the difference between mentors and sponsors. Mentors are members of your inner circle that you reach out to for advice. They provide you with guidance on what worked for them on their career path to show you a path to your goals. Mentors don't typically step in and make things happen, but rather are there to act as a sounding board for you to bring up ideas and suggestions, then provide feedback.

In the corporate world, sponsors are the golden key to advancement.

Sponsors are much bigger players in the game. This is where membership in the club begins to open doors for you. Sponsors are individuals that will nominate and support you for a role that perhaps you might not be 100 percent ready for. Sponsors have a belief in you. They stake their reputation on your performance. You don't seek a sponsor like you might a mentor. Instead, your results speak for themselves. Sponsors typically decide within the closed-door executive meetings if you are ready for promotion or advancement opportunities that include increased visibility and authority. Sponsors typically choose you to promote within the closed-door executive meetings for advancement opportunities with increased visibility and authority. Again, another great reason to join the club.

Leveraging your membership in the club doesn't stop at your company. To take it up a notch, the club can help you make a shift into a different company within your industry. After all, the network reaches far beyond your company.

Bold Move Option #2: Move into a New Industry

A second option is to take your skills, knowledge, and experience and transition into a new industry. This is a move that requires an amount of risk-taking. Entering a new industry is possible with the right preparation.

Start with where you want to go. If the industry you wish to pursue is similar to the one you are currently in, the transition is somewhat easier. For example, moving from commercial trucking into the automotive industry is relatively straightforward. Both are segments in the wider transportation sector, so there is overlap in process and product. Electronic control systems in a car are similar to those in a truck. The market, customer base, and competitive landscape differ, but with research you can get up to speed on what you need to know.

When your plan takes you to a completely new industry with little to no overlap, your transition will likely take more effort and time to complete. When I was in racing, it was difficult to imagine transitioning into a corporate-type role. The corporate job descriptions seemed so far from the roles and responsibilities as defined in professional motorsports. Most people saw racing as entertainment, not engineering or business development. At least that was my assumption.

After taking a detailed assessment of my responsibilities at the track, I recognized a pattern of experience that paralleled both motorsports and business. Teamwork, critical decision-making, superior communication skills, leadership, strategy, product development, quality and performance improvements, logistics, increasing revenue, brand awareness, regulations and compliance—the list went on. Wrapped in the disguise of professional motorsports was a gold mine of progressive leadership, engineering, and business management experiences that could easily translate into any corporate-type role. Over the years, I helped many of my racing colleagues successfully transition from a life on the road with the traveling circus of racing into a steady, corporate, 9-to-5 job to better fit their intended lifestyle. If veterans of a non-traditional job in racing can successfully reinvent themselves into a traditional corporate role, then you can go anywhere you want.

Most corporate women tend to focus their networking efforts internally, and you may have done that in the past as well. But, in order to move to a new industry, you must expand your network externally. Seek associations and conferences in the industry you wish to move into and start attending events. Be on the lookout for opportunities to assist others by utilizing your strengths, talents, and knowledge to build new relationships. At the same time, you will learn valuable insider information about the industry and the players that will be extremely helpful when an opportunity knocks. Also, keep clearly communicating where it is you want to go so people can assist in the transition. Focus on your strengths so that the fact you are a beginner in the new industry is not important.

Bold Move Option #3: Escape Corporate and Enter Entrepreneurship

Perhaps the boldest move of all in the terms of reinventing yourself is to become a corporate dropout and leap into entrepreneurship. Risk is high in this option, but with a well-thought-out strategy, calculated risk-taking, consistent action, and a team of supporters, this transition can be very successful.

This move definitely takes time, effort, and patience. Sure, you can go ahead and just quit your job tomorrow, but expect the process for building a successful business to be a lot more painful than if you had developed a plan while still employed. When you make the decision to strike out on your own, it is important to dream out loud. Allow yourself to hold the vision of where you want to go, then start talking to people and taking action.

When I work with clients on this bold transition, we start with developing a mindset built for success. There are always plenty of naysayers who want them not to change and stay right where they are. Having the confidence, clarity, and courage to keep moving forward when these negative influences approach is critical for success.

Go back and review chapter 3 on breaking through your inner glass ceiling. The most difficult obstacle you face in this option is the one you face in the mirror. Stay true to your vision and aligned with your values and nothing will stand in your way.

Escaping from corporate requires everything I have outlined thus far. To succeed, you must start with your inner game and playing to your strengths. Make sure your new business endeavor capitalizes on your unique assets. Start to research and follow others who run similar enterprises. Reach out to business owners through industry associations to gather information on market size, penetrability, competition, and opportunity. Understand exactly what you are getting yourself into. Be certain your new business not only fits your strengths, but also your values and priorities. Know that it might take longer than you expect to get your business up and running. Even the best-laid plans have hidden obstacles and challenges. But don't be discouraged. Instead reach out and find the support you need to take continual action. Begin with the end in mind, and develop your calculated risk plan.

Remind yourself that everyone started as a beginner. Even if you plan to move into consulting utilizing your experience from corporate, there will be a development time to establish systems, market yourself, and secure clients. Be confident in the fact you have been successful before. Give yourself permission to be patient and allow the right opportunities to unfold. High-achievers will get impatient with the progress of building a new business, especially when it appears to be moving slower than anticipated. Life as an entrepreneur is quite different from that of a corporate employee. In many ways too numerous and varied to list, the high risk is well worth the effort.

In the next chapters, I'll share how to make your bold move successful, sustainable, and lasting.

▶ FUEL FOR THOUGHT ◀

- For exponential growth and wealth, play to your strengths instead of focusing on fixing your weaknesses.

- You have essentially three options to reinvent yourself so that you fall in love with Monday mornings again.

- **Option #1:** Move within your company or industry by practicing self-promotion and leveraging your membership in the club.

- **Option #2:** Change industries by translating your top talents, skills, abilities, and experiences into transferable language appropriate for the new industry.

- **Option #3:** Escape corporate to enter entrepreneurship, but do your homework. Prepare a strategy for transition to be successful in taking what is considered the highest calculated risk in your career.

CHAPTER EIGHT

Build Your Winning Team

Keep away from people who try to belittle your ambitions. Small people always do that, but the really great ones make you feel that you too can become great.

MARK TWAIN

I n racing, although the driver receives the majority of the accolades, his ability to win is directly related to the team that surrounds him. Racing is a team sport. The truth is the driver could not possibly achieve winning results without the work, support, guidance, and strength of his team.

The same can be said about your career. Even though you individually take the bold actions to create the success you desire, you need a support team to provide advice, critical feedback, guidance, and support. This inner circle does not have to be large in number, but it does need to meet specific requirements.

Renowned businessman Jim Rohn once said, "You are the average of the five people you spend most of your time with." Bottom line: the people around you matter. You need people—mentors, coaches, colleagues, family, friends—who will challenge you and push you to become your best. Surround yourself with people who can run circles around you in as many areas as possible. When you engage with people who are exponentially better than you, the only result is that you will up-level yourself in the process. Your team should elevate your thinking and performance.

Negative People No More

In business, the team or department relationship is important to delivering results. Team members rely on one another to contribute and complete tasks. As a leader, you want a team that works well together while challenging one another to continually improve performance. When a team member is disengaged, she tends to pull down the energy of the remainder of the team. Productivity slows. If this pessimistic individual is not managed appropriately, the entire team's performance and attitude will suffer. Fortunately, there are corporate processes available to move an individual to another project or let them go. But how does one do that with members of their personal inner circle?

If you've ever been in a toxic environment—whether it's at work, in relationships, or friendships—you know how draining negative energy can be. It is important to stay away from the negative people who don't believe in your dream, pull you down, or hold you back. There are a lot of people that may appear like they want you to be successful, but deep down inside they don't want you to be any more successful than they are. Sometimes they can be close friends or colleagues at work. They're comfortable because you and they are both in the same place, and so just as long as you are within *their* comfort zone, they'll remain your friends and colleagues. However, once you start pushing outside your own comfort zone, the relationships begin to suffer.

As the leader of your career, you have some difficult choices to make. To achieve your goals, you have to weed out the folks that are dragging you down. You must decide if playing small to keep a friend is more important than stepping up into your power and blazing a trail that energizes and excites you. It's not always a draconian decision. As your success grows, your friend may see the positive impact your actions are making on your career and life and decide it's time to make changes as well. However, be aware that there will be some acquaintances that will not see the opportunity. Those are the ones you must let go of.

A Special Note on Family and Friends

For some, family and close friends are important to have in your inner circle. For me, my family and close friends provide insight and support like no one else. But I also know that they truly have my best interests at heart.

I want to make a suggestion here when you look to include family and friends in your inner circle. Unfortunately, I have seen many clients who believe their family is on their side, but cannot see the hidden agendas their friends and families have. You must understand the root of family and close friend support. Is a family member living vicariously through you and pushing you toward a career or decision that is against your priorities in order to fulfill some dream of theirs? Are they subtly holding you back by not supporting your goals and dreams so life and circumstances don't change? Even when change can mean greater prosperity and opportunity, change can be difficult for some to embrace. In close relationships, this can be difficult to see. As long as you stay clear and focused on *your* intentions, you can separate someone else's desires from your own.

In my inner circle, I have one close friend. She and I met early in my racing career and have remained friends and confidants for over eighteen years. She challenges me when doubt arises in me. Never has she tried to steer me in a particular direction, but instead listens and asks questions. When I ask for advice, she will give it to me straight—whether I like it or not. Her steady support has helped me through multiple career changes, divorce, loss, moving cross-country three times, and most recently leaving corporate to pursue entrepreneurship. I trust her instincts. I know she holds no hidden agendas (she openly tells me she wishes I lived closer, and I agree). Whenever I need guidance at a deep level, I call her. At times, she knows me better than I know myself. You need this type of friend on your team.

Take a close look at whom you hold close. Choose your inner circle wisely.

Who Needs to Be on Your Team?

You want to build a team of like-minded and positive, energetic people who will motivate, support, and guide you in your endeavors. Most importantly, particularly for women, your team needs to include both men and women. Be honest with yourself about how you feel about including both on your team since you could have a tendency to want to only collaborate with other women, believing that only women will understand your circumstances. But if you're really trying to make a difference and create the success you desire, it's imperative in this male-dominated culture that you have men on your team.

Why is this so important? Your team is there not only to guide you but also to give you critical feedback. This feedback is needed so you can make adjustments to keep moving forward. There are times when other women may just not see things the same way as men see them. Men bring a different perspective. Particularly if you're dealing with a move into a male-dominated discipline, company, or industry, it's crucial to know and understand the male perspective. How you interact is going to come across differently from a woman's perspective than from a man's perspective.

You want to have a well-rounded, diversified team. Team members should not all be your same age or at your same career level. Sure, you and your colleagues are experiencing similar things, but you also need advice from individuals who have traveled the path before you. Reach out to people who are more successful than you. Take a look at where you want to go next, and seek out the advice of the person who currently holds that role. You might learn some insider secrets to make that move faster.

Your inner circle carries the responsibilities similar to that of a board of directors or a team of advisors. When a company assembles its board of directors, it builds a cross-functional team to provide input and advice from various areas. For instance, you don't want all finance people on the board of a manufacturing company, and you don't want all marketing people on the board of a service business. The same holds true for your team. You want to make sure you have cross-functional representation, especially if your bold move entails moving to new industries or functional areas. Reach out to those who are well connected and develop a relationship.

Another key team member is a professional coach. The right coach can provide you with objective perspective on your situation. The coaching modality is meant to improve your performance by helping you bridge the gap between where you are now and where you want to be. So, when planning a career move, having a coach on your team can be constructive. Find a coach that fits your personality and has experience helping others achieve similar goals that you have. Accountability is critical to keep you focused and advancing. Your coach can be your accountability partner and biggest cheerleader.

When the Team Needs to Change

It's likely you will not have the same team, or inner circle, throughout your entire career. Your goals and ambitions change. As a result, the support team you have may also need to change. A good example is when you make the decision to leave corporate and pursue entrepreneurship.

When I took the leap from corporate, not many in my network knew my intentions ahead of time. My family and a few select close friends were the only ones that knew of my entrepreneurial plans. Needless to say, a few months after leaving, I felt alone in my business. The colleagues I had from my previous life in corporate did not quite understand what I was trying to accomplish. I desperately needed a new support team.

I was introduced to the centuries-old concept of a mastermind. Essentially, it is very similar to your inner circle. The idea is that multiple minds put together are more powerful than one alone. Napoleon Hill discusses the concept of masterminds in great detail in his book, *Think and Grow Rich*. "No individual has sufficient experience, education, native ability, and knowledge to ensure the accumulation of a great fortune without the cooperation of other people."

For some reason, in the corporate world, this concept is not common in the middle ranks. At the C-Suite level, many executives do participate in a mastermind group outside of their own company. Vistage is an example of an organized mastermind community. Their mission is to help CEOs and executives grow their businesses by making better decisions and achieving better results.

As I continued to work on building my business, I came across many potential mentors to support my work. However, I found one mentor that resonated with me more than others. I knew I needed to develop more structures to build the foundation of my business, and I also knew I needed a support team to help guide me through the process. I joined my mentor's mastermind group to take my business to the next level. The group was exactly what I needed as my new team—entrepreneurs at various stages of development working together to up-level their business.

The impact has been phenomenal. My team is full of entrepreneurs who challenge my limiting beliefs and push me beyond my comfort zone. They are available for critical feedback and brainstorming new ideas. An added benefit is the potential for collaboration on future projects. My goals and ambition have changed from my corporate track. This new mastermind team is exactly what I needed to bring into my world to support my new direction.

The goal of your team, whether it is a corporate inner circle or an entrepreneurial mastermind group, is to get feedback from trusted advisors that you respect and who care about your success. This feedback will provide you the fuel to break through what's holding you back, open up new possibilities, and encourage you to take the risks needed to create success on your terms.

▶ FUEL FOR THOUGHT ◀

- Everyone needs a support team to provide advice, critical feedback, guidance, and support.

- Remove the team members who hold you back or weigh you down.

- Build your team with people more successful than you, and make sure you include men.

- When your goals change, your team might need to change. Be aware of that and make sure your support is aligned with your ambition.

CHAPTER NINE

Invest in Yourself

It's not always possible to be the best, but it is always possible to improve your own performance.

JACKIE STEWART

What is more important than joining the club, taking more risks, reinventing yourself, and building your winning support team? Continually investing in yourself to improve your knowledge, talents, and abilities to perform at your peak potential. A beautiful flower may bloom, but without continuous sunlight, water, and food, it will wither and die. Continual feeding is required for additional growth. When you choose not to take action on personal or professional growth opportunities, you stagnate. The choice of inaction creates complacency and expands the boundaries of your comfort zone. Actively choosing to invest in yourself continuously works to break down those boundaries so you continue to grow.

Corporate America promotes a false sense of security. As part of your leadership-development plan, the company may send you to training and development courses. Typically, these courses are chosen based on the needs of the company, not necessarily what is in your best interests for professional growth. By all means, take advantage of the offerings your company provides. However, you must also make sure you are getting the education, training, and support that you need as an individual to succeed and perform at your peak.

It's often the case that a problem arises when leadership at the company changes. Suddenly, the direction of the company and its development of personnel can change. The skills and training that were important to the previous management team are not valued by the new management team. You may question whether or not you are still on the leadership track. Politics shift the landscape, and if you are not prepared, the results can be devastating to your development and advancement opportunities.

Another potential issue is shifts in the overall economic climate. If the company needs to cut costs to remain profitable, one expense that is typically cut is training and development. It's unfortunate, but true. People development, in most corporate environments, is put aside when the shareholders demand profits. The short-term gains are more important in economic slowdowns than the long-term development strategy is. You can see how relying solely on the development programs offered by your company can leave you out in the cold.

By taking your career development into your own hands, you can make sure you get what you need. This allows you to remain nimble in the face of change. You consistently enhance your talents and build your strengths to utilize within your company, industry, or elsewhere if you choose to pursue new paths. So, get off of cruise control and take back the wheel of your career.

Methods of Investment

Legendary investor Warren Buffett said, "Investing in yourself is the best thing you can do. Anything that improves your own talents; nobody can tax it or take it away from you. They can run up huge deficits and the dollar can become worth far less. You can have all kinds of things happen. But if you've got talent yourself, and you've maximized your talent, you've got a tremendous asset that can return ten-fold."

There are many different ways you can choose to invest in yourself. An easy one is to read books on leadership, business, or a particular area of interest that is directly related to the direction you want your career to grow. For example, if you know you need to become a better communicator, seek information and books that teach you tools and strategies you can implement. Industry-specific trade publications are a great source of information and possibly new opportunities. Mainstream magazines, such as *Forbes*, *Entrepreneur*, and *Inc.*, may also open your mind to new ideas, concepts, and strategies for your career and business.

Another great suggestion is to enroll in professional development courses. There are so many offerings, both online and offline, that provide immense value to your growth. You can find courses specific to your industry or discipline to enhance your knowledge. Check out your local community college for ideas as well. Increasing your knowledge through courses and training is ideal if you're seeking new challenges in different industries and especially if you're longing to leave corporate and enter entrepreneurship.

Invest in yourself by attending industry conferences. Many times you can leverage your current position within your company to attend specific industry conferences within your area of expertise. For instance, many engineers in the automotive and commercial trucking industry attend the Society of Automotive Engineers National Conference. By attending industry conferences you can gain new insights in your specific area of expertise. You can also leverage your time at the conference to build your network and increase your influence. Perhaps you learn of a great new approach you can bring back to your team for implementation. Even if you have to pay for the conference yourself, there are numerous ways to see that return on your investment.

Investing in yourself does not always have to be professional in nature. Personal development is just as important in your career advancement. Joining Toastmasters to improve your public speaking and presentation skills will greatly help your confidence in front of groups. A course on internal mindset strategies can help you overcome those inner obstacles getting in your way. Programs on time management and goal setting can keep you moving forward in action. Don't forget your health and wellness on this journey either.

The key here is to make sure you're investing in yourself continuously, even when someone is or isn't footing the bill. Find creative ways to build and expand your abilities. Leverage programs offered through your industry associations and networking groups. Invest your time to attend lectures and panel discussions and open your mind to new possibilities. While you are there, start up conversations. You just never know where a conversation may lead.

Perhaps the best investment I've seen many mid-career women and executives take is investing in a professional coach. Many executives have professional coaches to improve their performance, keep them accountable, and push them to reach new heights in their careers. Working in partnership with a coach, people accomplish more (and faster) than they would have on their own. Just as athletes use a coach to maximize their efforts and reach their peak performance, a coach can assist you in developing the skills you already possess to create more wins in your career and life. What do you stand to gain when working with a professional coach? The possibilities are endless.

▶ **You take yourself more seriously.** Investing in your professional and personal growth sends a powerful message to the world that you are serious about moving ahead. When you make that commitment to yourself, amazing things start to happen.

▶ **You gain more clarity in your business and professional life.** People who are scattered cannot move forward. They paralyze themselves. Get clear on your goals in business and life to take the right actions to achieve success. The right coach will get you focused on what is most important to you.

▶ **You are exposed to new business techniques.** Coaches work with individuals and businesses across disciplines and industries. As a result, you learn from their vast experience, knowledge, and understanding of best practices. Ideas, solutions, and outside perspectives might be exactly what you need for your next breakthrough.

▶ **You eliminate self-defeating thought patterns and habits.** Your toughest critic is *you*. A skilled coach will help you to identify when you are beating yourself up and provide you with strategies and tools to eliminate your self-doubt.

▶ **You become a more powerful communicator.**
Powerful communication is about being specific and
direct. Build your influence and reach as a leader by
refining your message. A coach will help you create a
clear and powerful message.

▶ **You make and keep more money.** The old
adage—"To make money you must spend money"—is
true. Investing in yourself through coaching is the *best*
money spent. The right coach will help you increase
your earnings and create financial freedom.

▶ **You have more time, energy, and satisfaction.**
Who doesn't want more time, energy, and satisfaction
in life? Coaching clears the clutter that's weighing you
down so you can create the career and life you truly
desire. That includes spending time the way you want,
increasing your energy levels for those things most
important to you, and finding sustainable happiness.

▶ **You find and fuel your passion.** Your passion is
that inner fire that's burning inside—yes, you know
the one. The right coach will not only identify that fire
but also guide you in adding fuel to your passion and
creating the career, business, and life that feeds that
inner fire for years to come.

With all these amazing possibilities available, what
are you waiting for? Many coaches offer introductory
sessions so you can try coaching out before making a

bigger commitment. You owe it to yourself to imagine the potential.

If you are feeling inspired to create success in your career and life, I invite you to join the F.A.S.T. Women in Business community and find out how you and I can work together more closely to achieve your career and business dreams.

To fall in love with Monday mornings again and create the wildly successful career and life you desire isn't about luck—it's a decision. It happens every day. Why not you? Why not now? Make the decision to go *F.A.S.T.*

► FUEL FOR THOUGHT ◄

- Invest in yourself to improve your knowledge, talents, and abilities to perform at your peak potential.

- Don't rely solely on the training and development offered at your company.

- Read books, attend conferences, and take new courses to enhance your professional and personal growth.

- The best investment you can make in yourself is to hire a professional coach. Working in partnership with a coach, people accomplish more than they would have on their own and faster.

APPENDIX A

About the Author

Nadine Haupt is a pioneer for women in traditionally male-dominated technical fields and an expert in how to succeed in them. As a professional coach and consultant, Nadine helps individuals accelerate their impact, influence, and income to create success and wealth on their terms by transforming their approach to leadership. Nadine is also an insightful professional speaker delivering high-energy, high-content programs at corporate, small business, and association events across the globe.

Since 1994, Nadine blazed a successful trail from pit lane to the corporate boardroom—including becoming the first female trackside engineer in IndyCar racing—navigating the twists and turns of start-ups, niche businesses, consulting firms, and corporations. Nadine has been featured on ABC, ESPN, ESPN2, and PBS, in addition to domestic and foreign newspapers. Her expertise, business success, and devotion to mentoring women recently earned her nominations for both the 2014 and 2015 Influential Woman in Trucking Award.

Nadine is the founder and Chief Empowerment Officer of F.A.S.T. Women in Business—the preeminent coaching and consulting firm dedicated to helping motivated women ignite their passion, create success and wealth on their terms, and become Fearless, Ambitious, Strong, and Trailblazing (F.A.S.T.). Nadine's clients are drawn to her passion, authenticity, professionalism, and down-to-earth style. Her no-nonsense approach challenges clients while her compassion and support encourages them to make bold moves.

Nadine has a bachelor of science in mechanical engineering from Purdue University, a master of science in mechanical engineering from Oakland University, a master of material science engineering from Illinois Institute of Technology, and a master of business administration from the Graziadio School of Business and Management at Pepperdine University. In addition to her licensure as a professional engineer, she also holds an Associate Coaching Certification from the International Coach Federation, Certified Professional Coach and Energy Leadership Index – Master Practitioner certifications from the Institute of Professional Excellence in Coaching, and a certificate in Non-Profit Management from the University of Illinois – Chicago. Nadine currently serves on the Board of both the National Speakers Association – Illinois Chapter and the Purdue University Engineering Alumni Association.

When she is not motivating and inspiring audiences with her speaking or coaching clients to greatness, Nadine enjoys tent camping, hiking, and seeking new adventures with her copilot, Lucy—a rescued eleven year old Korean Jindo mix pup who also serves as the F.A.S.T. Women in Business "Chief Motivating Officer." She and Lucy reside in the Chicago metropolitan area.

APPENDIX B

Acknowledgments

If someone had said to me a year ago that I would write and publish a book, I would have laughed. I'm a speaker and coach, not a writer. Sure I had thoughts in my head, but no real plan to get them down on paper. From beginning to end of this journey, it has been a team effort. Without the guidance, support, and encouragement from my winning team, this book would not be a reality.

To my publishing team at Indie Books International: Mark LeBlanc opened my eyes to the impact writing a book would make in growing my business. Henry DeVries strategized with me to structure my book effectively and efficiently while providing the guidance I needed to stay on track and get it done. As my developmental editor, Henry's valuable feedback on the manuscript sharpened my message with focus and clarity. Henry really is the "Book Doctor." Devin DeVries guided me through the editing and layout process. No small task when dealing with a first-time author.

Gratitude and love to Ingrid Elfver and Mark Malatesta of Born Celebrity. Your vision and creative energy birthed my personal brand of F.A.S.T. Women in Business. I would not have the success mindset and the framework of my business without you both. Your steadfast belief in me has allowed me to powerfully step into my greatness with confidence and authenticity.

To my parents, Jim and Betty – thank you for your enduring and loving support of the crazy things I choose to do in life (and there have been a few). You taught me that when I have faith and believe in myself, I could achieve anything. You have nurtured my passion, celebrated my success, and comforted me in defeat. For that, and so much more, I am forever grateful.

To my sister, Heather – you have always been my biggest cheerleader. Thank you for continually encouraging me to reach for my dreams. You inspire me to embrace life with love and passion each and every day.

To my best friend, Lucy – you have been faithfully by my side for over eleven years and always up for a new adventure. Thanks for your unconditional love and gentle nudges to encourage me to go for a walk when I was working too hard. I'll grab your leash. Meet me at the door.

20736943R00075

Made in the USA
Middletown, DE
07 June 2015